Copyright © 2020 Sarah Yakawonis

Imprint: Independently published

Sarah Yakawonis

Tacoma, WA 98466

Designed by: Sarah Yakawonis

lustrations by: Sarah Yakawonis and Lana Elanor in collaboration

ISBN: 9798607257033

MANIFEST
ABUNDANCE

A journal to practice manifesting abundance and
cultivate a deeper understanding of the law of attraction

by Sarah Yakawonis

Intro

I have been interested in magic and manifestation for my whole life. About ten years ago, I started to study the Law of Attraction. I've read every self-help book I can get my hands on, I've watched YouTube and documentaries, I've take IRL and online workshops, and I've practiced (at least for a little while) much of what I've been introduced to. I believe that the law of attraction works for everyone, but the same techniques don't work the same for everyone. It's like a key. You have to find your perfect fit. The information that lights you up, the meditation techniques that connect you to greatness, the journaling prompts that create those amazing feelings that can't help but become an amazing reality.

For me, journaling works really well. It's one of my keys. And that's why I've designed this journal. It's a fast, easy way for me to practice getting in tune with those high vibe feelings! I figure that there are other seekers and lightworkers out there who would benefit from this simple practice too! Because at the end of the day, I'm just a seeker like you. Except I have a BFA in graphic design, so I could make this journal. But honestly, I know how this journal really came about, you and everyone else who bought this book manifested it so that you could raise your vibration and practice manifestation too. So truly, way to go, you did it!

Practice

This journal is designed for practicing the art of manifestation. Practice being the keyword, because with practice comes progress. You can't become a world-class athlete by sitting on the couch, watching ESPN. You have to get up and practice.

How to use this journal

1) Begin with a little meditation, bath, or workout. However, you find those high vibing feelings.
2) Now turn to the first page with a heart and write something that you love and appreciate. Don't fill out the whole page, just the top.
3) Think of something else you love and appreciate and write that on the top of the next page with a hart. Continue doing this for about 20 min, or it stops feeling good.
4) Skip the manifestation pages for now.
5) Go back to the first page, and in the "because" section, writes all of the reasons you love and appreciate it.

On the pages with hearts

Start by writing something you love and appreciate. It could be. . .

Δ Someone you love

Δ a Pet

Δ a favorite thing

Δ a place you love to visit

Δ a something from your past

Δ something you love to use

Δ something you love to do

Δ a show

Δ music

Δ your favorite foods

Δ celebrities

Δ books

Δ spirituality

Δ **Or literally, ANYTHING that exists or did exist and that you have for yourself experienced.**

Now write why you love it in the "because" section. If you get stuck, try these prompts.

Δ Why do you like it so much?

Δ Why do you love it?

Δ Is it visually appealing? How So?

Δ Does it taste/smell good? How so?

Δ How does it feel to be around it/them?

On the pages with the moons

In much the same way we wrote things we love and why we love them. On the manifestation pages, write what you desire to create under "I'm creating the momentum to manifest". In the "because" section, write why you want it to have it be a part of your experience!
Δ What will you do with it?
Δ Why do you want it?
Δ How will it benefit you?
Δ How will it benefit your family?
Δ How will it benefit others?
Δ How would it feel to have it?

I designed this page with moons as a gentle reminder that manifesting things sometimes will take a little time to align. It will happen as naturally as the phases of the moon, and just like them, it can't be rushed.

Why it works

I think this journal is so powerful because it raises your vibration by loving and appreciating your experience. It also treats what you would like to be in your experience and what is in your experience nearly identically, really bringing the vibration of what does exists and what does not closer together! By loving and appreciating all that is, you really do create the momentum to manifest your dream life! Or maybe something even better!

I love and appreciate

Because

I love and appreciate

Because

I love and appreciate

Because

I'm creating the momentum to manifest

Because

Or **maybe** something even better!

I love and appreciate

Because

I love and appreciate

Because

I love and appreciate _____

Because _____

I'm creating the momentum to manifest

Because

Or **maybe** something even better!

I love and appreciate

Because

I love and appreciate

Because

I love and appreciate

Because

I'm creating the momentum to manifest

Because

Or **maybe** something even better!

I love and appreciate

Because

I love and appreciate

Because

I love and appreciate

Because

I'm creating the momentum to manifest

Because

Or **maybe** something even better!

I love and appreciate _____

_____

_____

_____

Because _____

_____

_____

_____

_____

_____

_____

_____

_____

_____

_____

_____

_____

_____

_____

_____

_____

_____

_____

_____

I love and appreciate _____

_____

_____

_____

Because _____

_____

_____

_____

_____

_____

_____

_____

_____

_____

_____

_____

_____

_____

_____

_____

_____

_____

I love and appreciate

Because

I'm creating the momentum to manifest

Because

Or **maybe** something even better!

I love and appreciate

Because

I love and appreciate _____

_____

_____

_____

_____

Because _____

_____

_____

_____

_____

_____

_____

_____

_____

_____

_____

_____

_____

_____

_____

_____

_____

_____

_____

I love and appreciate

Because

I'm creating the momentum to manifest

Because

Or **maybe** something even better!

I love and appreciate

Because

I love and appreciate

Because

I love and appreciate

Because

I'm creating the momentum to manifest

Because

Or **maybe** something even better!

I love and appreciate

Because

I love and appreciate

Because

I love and appreciate

Because

I'm creating the momentum to manifest

Because

Or **maybe** something even better!

I love and appreciate _____

_____

_____

_____

Because _____

_____

_____

_____

_____

_____

_____

_____

_____

_____

_____

_____

_____

_____

_____

_____

_____

_____

_____

I love and appreciate

Because

I love and appreciate

Because

I'm creating the momentum to manifest

Because

Or **maybe** something even better!

I love and appreciate

Because

I love and appreciate _____

_____

_____

_____

_____

Because _____

_____

_____

_____

_____

_____

_____

_____

_____

_____

_____

_____

_____

_____

_____

_____

_____

_____

_____

_____

_____

_____

I love and appreciate

Because

I'm creating the momentum to manifest

Because

Or **maybe** something even better!

I love and appreciate _____

_____

_____

_____

Because _____

_____

_____

_____

_____

_____

_____

_____

_____

_____

_____

_____

_____

_____

_____

_____

_____

_____

_____

I love and appreciate

Because

I love and appreciate

Because

I'm creating the momentum to manifest

Because

Or **maybe** something even better!

I love and appreciate

Because

I love and appreciate _____

_____

_____

_____

_____

Because _____

_____

_____

_____

_____

_____

_____

_____

_____

_____

_____

_____

_____

_____

_____

_____

_____

_____

_____

_____

_____

I love and appreciate

Because

I'm creating the momentum to manifest

Because

Or **maybe** something even better!

I love and appreciate

Because

I love and appreciate _____

_____

_____

_____

_____

Because _____

_____

_____

_____

_____

_____

_____

_____

_____

_____

_____

_____

_____

_____

_____

_____

_____

_____

_____

I love and appreciate

Because

I'm creating the momentum to manifest

Because

Or **maybe** something even better!

I love and appreciate _____

_____

_____

_____

Because _____

_____

_____

_____

_____

_____

_____

_____

_____

_____

_____

_____

_____

_____

_____

_____

_____

_____

_____

_____

I love and appreciate _____

_____

_____

_____

Because _____

I love and appreciate

Because

I'm creating the momentum to manifest

Because

Or **maybe** something even better!

I love and appreciate

Because

I love and appreciate

Because

I love and appreciate

Because

I'm creating the momentum to manifest

Because

Or **maybe** something even better!

I love and appreciate

Because

I love and appreciate

Because

I love and appreciate

Because

I'm creating the momentum to manifest

Because

Or **maybe** something even better!

I love and appreciate _____

_____

_____

_____

Because _____

_____

_____

_____

_____

_____

_____

_____

_____

_____

_____

_____

_____

_____

_____

_____

_____

_____

_____

_____

I love and appreciate

Because

I love and appreciate

Because

I'm creating the momentum to manifest

Because

Or **maybe** something even better!

I love and appreciate

Because

I love and appreciate

Because

I love and appreciate

Because

I'm creating the momentum to manifest

Because

Or **maybe** something even better!

I love and appreciate

Because

I love and appreciate

Because

I love and appreciate

Because

I'm creating the momentum to manifest

Because

Or **maybe** something even better!

I love and appreciate _____

Because _____

I love and appreciate

Because

I love and appreciate

Because

I'm creating the momentum to manifest

Because

Or **maybe** something even better!

I love and appreciate

Because

I love and appreciate

Because

I love and appreciate

Because

I'm creating the momentum to manifest

Because

Or **maybe** something even better!

I love and appreciate

Because

I love and appreciate

Because

I love and appreciate

Because

I'm creating the momentum to manifest

Because

Or **maybe** something even better!

I love and appreciate _____

_____

_____

_____

Because _____

_____

_____

_____

_____

_____

_____

_____

_____

_____

_____

_____

_____

_____

_____

_____

_____

_____

_____

_____

I love and appreciate

Because

I love and appreciate

Because

I'm creating the momentum to manifest

Because

Or **maybe** something even better!

I love and appreciate

Because

I love and appreciate

Because

I love and appreciate

Because

I'm creating the momentum to manifest

Because

Or **maybe** something even better!

I love and appreciate

Because

I love and appreciate

Because

I love and appreciate

Because

I'm creating the momentum to manifest

Because

Or **maybe** something even better!

I love and appreciate

Because

I love and appreciate

Because

I love and appreciate

Because

I'm creating the momentum to manifest

Because

Or **maybe** something even better!

I love and appreciate

Because

I love and appreciate

Because

I love and appreciate

Because

I'm creating the momentum to manifest

Because

Or **maybe** something even better!

I love and appreciate

Because

I love and appreciate _____

_____

_____

_____

_____

Because _____

_____

_____

_____

_____

_____

_____

_____

_____

_____

_____

_____

_____

_____

_____

_____

_____

_____

_____

_____

_____

_____

I love and appreciate

Because

I'm creating the momentum to manifest

Because

Or **maybe** something even better!

I love and appreciate

_____

Because

I love and appreciate

Because

I love and appreciate

Because

I'm creating the momentum to manifest

Because

Or **maybe** something even better!

I love and appreciate _____

_____

_____

_____

Because _____

_____

_____

_____

_____

_____

_____

_____

_____

_____

_____

_____

_____

_____

_____

_____

_____

_____

_____

_____

I love and appreciate

Because

I love and appreciate

Because

I'm creating the momentum to manifest

Because

Or **maybe** something even better!

I love and appreciate

Because

I love and appreciate

Because

I love and appreciate

Because

I'm creating the momentum to manifest

Because

Or **maybe** something even better!

I love and appreciate _____

_____

_____

_____

Because _____

_____

_____

_____

_____

_____

_____

_____

_____

_____

_____

_____

_____

_____

_____

_____

_____

_____

_____

_____

I love and appreciate _____

_____

_____

_____

Because _____

_____

_____

_____

_____

_____

_____

_____

_____

_____

_____

_____

_____

_____

_____

_____

_____

_____

_____

_____

_____

I love and appreciate

Because

I'm creating the momentum to manifest

Because

Or **maybe** something even better!

I love and appreciate

Because

I love and appreciate _____

_____

_____

_____

Because _____

_____

_____

_____

_____

_____

_____

_____

_____

_____

_____

_____

_____

_____

_____

_____

_____

_____

_____

I love and appreciate

Because

I'm creating the momentum to manifest

Because

Or **maybe** something even better!

I love and appreciate _____

_____
_____
_____

Because _____
_____
_____
_____
_____
_____
_____
_____
_____
_____
_____
_____
_____
_____
_____
_____
_____
_____
_____
_____
_____

I love and appreciate

Because

I love and appreciate

Because

I'm creating the momentum to manifest

Because

Or **maybe** something even better!

I love and appreciate _____

_____

_____

_____

Because _____

_____

_____

_____

_____

_____

_____

_____

_____

_____

_____

_____

_____

_____

_____

_____

_____

_____

_____

_____

I love and appreciate

_____

_____

_____

_____

Because

_____

_____

_____

_____

_____

_____

_____

_____

_____

_____

_____

_____

_____

_____

_____

_____

_____

_____

_____

_____

I love and appreciate

Because

I'm creating the momentum to manifest

Because

Or **maybe** something even better!

I love and appreciate _____

_____
_____
_____
_____

Because _____

_____
_____
_____
_____
_____
_____
_____
_____
_____
_____
_____
_____
_____
_____
_____
_____
_____
_____
_____
_____

I love and appreciate

Because

I love and appreciate

Because

I'm creating the momentum to manifest

Because

Or **maybe** something even better!

I love and appreciate _____

_____

_____

_____

_____

Because _____

_____

_____

_____

_____

_____

_____

_____

_____

_____

_____

_____

_____

_____

_____

_____

_____

_____

_____

_____

_____

_____

_____

I love and appreciate _____

_____

_____

_____

Because _____

_____

_____

_____

_____

_____

_____

_____

_____

_____

_____

_____

_____

_____

_____

_____

_____

I love and appreciate

Because

I'm creating the momentum to manifest

Because

Or **maybe** something even better!

I love and appreciate

Because

I love and appreciate

Because

I love and appreciate _____

_____

_____

_____

Because _____

_____

_____

_____

_____

_____

_____

_____

_____

_____

_____

_____

_____

_____

_____

_____

_____

_____

_____

_____

_____

I'm creating the momentum to manifest

Because

Or **maybe** something even better!

I love and appreciate _____

_____

_____

_____

Because _____

_____

_____

_____

_____

_____

_____

_____

_____

_____

_____

_____

_____

_____

_____

_____

_____

_____

_____

_____

_____

_____

I love and appreciate

Because

I love and appreciate

Because

I'm creating the momentum to manifest

Because

Or **maybe** something even better!

I love and appreciate

Because

I love and appreciate _____

_____

_____

_____

Because _____

_____

_____

_____

_____

_____

_____

_____

_____

_____

_____

_____

_____

_____

_____

_____

_____

I love and appreciate

Because

I'm creating the momentum to manifest

Because

Or **maybe** something even better!

I love and appreciate _____

_____

_____

_____

Because _____

_____

_____

_____

_____

_____

_____

_____

_____

_____

_____

_____

_____

_____

_____

_____

_____

_____

_____

I love and appreciate

Because

I love and appreciate

Because

I'm creating the momentum to manifest

Because

Or **maybe** something even better!

I love and appreciate _____

_____

_____

_____

Because _____

_____

_____

_____

_____

_____

_____

_____

_____

_____

_____

_____

_____

_____

_____

_____

_____

_____

_____

_____

_____

_____

I love and appreciate

Because

I love and appreciate

Because

I'm creating the momentum to manifest

Because

Or **maybe** something even better!

I love and appreciate

Because

I love and appreciate _____

_____

_____

_____

Because _____

_____

_____

_____

_____

_____

_____

_____

_____

_____

_____

_____

_____

_____

_____

_____

_____

I love and appreciate

Because

I'm creating the momentum to manifest

Because

Or **maybe** something even better!

I love and appreciate _____

_____

_____

_____

Because _____

_____

_____

_____

_____

_____

_____

_____

_____

_____

_____

_____

_____

_____

_____

_____

_____

_____

_____

_____

I love and appreciate

Because

I love and appreciate

Because

I'm creating the momentum to manifest

Because

Or **maybe** something even better!

I love and appreciate
_____

_____

_____

_____

Because
_____

_____

_____

_____

_____

_____

_____

_____

_____

_____

_____

_____

_____

_____

_____

_____

_____

_____

_____

I love and appreciate _____

Because _____

I love and appreciate

Because

I'm creating the momentum to manifest

Because

Or **maybe** something even better!

I love and appreciate _____

_____

_____

_____

Because _____

_____

_____

_____

_____

_____

_____

_____

_____

_____

_____

_____

_____

_____

_____

_____

_____

_____

_____

_____

_____

_____

I love and appreciate

Because

I love and appreciate

Because

I'm creating the momentum to manifest

Because

Or **maybe** something even better!

I love and appreciate _____

_____

_____

_____

_____

Because _____

_____

_____

_____

_____

_____

_____

_____

_____

_____

_____

_____

_____

_____

_____

_____

_____

_____

_____

_____

_____

I love and appreciate

Because

I love and appreciate

Because

I'm creating the momentum to manifest

Because

Or **maybe** something even better!

I love and appreciate _____

_____

_____

_____

Because _____

_____

_____

_____

_____

_____

_____

_____

_____

_____

_____

_____

_____

_____

_____

_____

_____

_____

_____

_____

_____

I love and appreciate

Because

I love and appreciate

Because

I'm creating the momentum to manifest

Because

Or **maybe** something even better!

I love and appreciate

Because

I love and appreciate

Because

I love and appreciate

Because

I'm creating the momentum to manifest

Because

Or **maybe** something even better!

I love and appreciate

Because

I love and appreciate

Because

<u>I love and appreciate</u>

<u>Because</u>

I'm creating the momentum to manifest

Because

Or **maybe** something even better!

I love and appreciate

_____

_____

_____

Because

_____

_____

_____

_____

_____

_____

_____

_____

_____

_____

_____

_____

_____

_____

_____

_____

_____

_____

_____

_____

_____

_____

I love and appreciate

Because

I love and appreciate

Because

I'm creating the momentum to manifest

Because

Or **maybe** something even better!

I love and appreciate

Because

I love and appreciate

Because

I love and appreciate _____

_____

_____

_____

Because _____

_____

_____

_____

_____

_____

_____

_____

_____

_____

_____

_____

_____

_____

_____

_____

_____

_____

_____

_____

_____

I'm creating the momentum to manifest

Because

Or **maybe** something even better!

I love and appreciate

Because

I love and appreciate

Because

I love and appreciate

Because

I'm creating the momentum to manifest

Because

Or **maybe** something even better!

I love and appreciate _____

_____

_____

_____

Because _____

_____

_____

_____

_____

_____

_____

_____

_____

_____

_____

_____

_____

_____

_____

_____

_____

_____

_____

_____

_____

_____

I love and appreciate

Because

I love and appreciate

Because

I'm creating the momentum to manifest

Because

Or **maybe** something even better!

What did you manifest?

Look through this journal and use these pages to document what you manifested!

_____

_____

_____

_____

_____

_____

_____

_____

_____

_____

_____

_____

_____

_____

_____

_____

_____

_____

_____

_____

_____

_____

_____

_____

_____

Made in the USA
Monee, IL
11 September 2020